Time's Up

"The museum will close in 20 minutes," a recorded voice announced.

"I'll never finish this museum hunt in 20 minutes!" Marisa wailed. Ms. Baker, her teacher, had given the class an assignment to find and write one fact about 50 different historic artifacts during their afternoon trip to the Museum of Natural History.

"I only have five more things to find," her friend Will said.

"I have ten," Marisa whined.

"You still have ten? I told you not to spend so much time at the dolphin exhibit," he said.

"I know, but I love dolphins," she said. Marisa had that pleading expression that she always used when she wanted Will to help her.

"Come on. We'll have to hurry if you're going to find ten more things," he said, impatiently.

"Look over here," Marisa said as she stopped in front of a display case. She pointed to a deerskin dress made by an Iroquois woman. "Wow! Look at all that beadwork. I wish I had a dress like that," she sighed in a dreamy voice.

"It's a wedding dress," Will told her as he read from the sign next to the case. They both checked the item on their lists and wrote the fact, "This is a wedding dress," next to "Iroquois beaded dress" on their papers.

Frantically searching for other things on their list, Marisa and Will then hurried through the museum. They had soon left behind their class group and their teacher. They went downstairs and raced through the Hall of Ocean Life where they wrote a fact about a giant squid suspended from the ceiling. In the Hall of Primates they recorded a fact about great apes. They still needed information about the reptile and dinosaur exhibits, so they went back upstairs and continued from room to room, checking off more things on their lists as they went.

"It's nearly closing time," a guard warned as Marisa and Will approached a life-sized model of a *Tyrannosaurus rex.*

"Thanks. We're going," Marisa replied.

"I'm done!" Will announced as he wrote down, "*T. rex* was a meat eater."

"I'm not," Marisa said, glancing over at his list. "I still have five more things to find."

He read her list. "I found four of the things you need in the Hall of . . . ."

"The museum closes in five minutes. Please go to the front entrance," a recording said.

"We'd better leave now so we can find the rest of our class," Will said, looking around. "We were supposed to stay with them."

"No, no," Marisa insisted. "I need to cross off these last five things."

"We'll pass the Hall of African Mammals on the way out," Will said. "You'll find some of the stuff you need there." They took the elevator to the first floor and walked quickly to the exhibit.

"Hurry up!" Will urged.

"I'm coming," Marisa replied breathlessly, as she walked faster.

Stopping to look at a display showing a herd of zebras grazing on a rolling, grassy plain, Will said, "Everything looks so real. It's almost as if I'm really in Africa watching zebras." Wishing he could truly be there, he stood gazing at the display for a moment. Then he turned to Marisa, but he didn't see her.

"Marisa?" he called softly.

Chapter 2

Locked In

Will didn't hear anything, so he called Marisa's name again, this time a little louder. Just as he began to panic, he heard, "I'm over here." At first, he couldn't tell where she was calling from, so he began walking slowly around the room. Then he heard Marisa's voice emerging from behind a hut constructed of mud and sticks.

Will leaned over the velvet ropes surrounding the display. "Where are you?" he hissed.

"Back here," she answered.

Will carefully stepped over the ropes and walked toward the back of the hut. He found her crouched over a plaque next to the hut. "You're not supposed to be back here," he informed her as he looked over her shoulder.

"I know, but it's hard to see everything from behind the ropes," Marisa replied, copying a fact from the sign. "It's so much better to get a close-up look. It's almost real when you're not looking at the ropes."

Just then, a guard entered the hall. Marisa crouched down, pulling Will after her so the guard wouldn't see that they were inside the ropes. The guard surveyed the room for any lingering visitors and walked out.

"We have to go," Will hissed.

"Let's go to the Hall of Precious Gems. I have to find a piece of crystal, and I bet there's one there," said Marisa.

"It's there because I saw it already," Will told her, "but we don't have time because the museum is closing right now." He was beginning to panic.

Marisa headed down the hallway. "It will take forever to close down a place this huge," she said, casually. "We have plenty of time."

Will hurried alongside her. "Okay, I'll show you exactly where it is so you don't waste time searching for it. Then we have to find the class."

"Thanks," Marisa said, as they went upstairs and entered the Hall of Precious Gems.

After Will showed her where to find the crystal, it took only a minute for her to write down an additional fact. That was one minute too long for Will.

Once again, a recording announced, "The Museum of Natural History is now closing. Thank you and come again."

"We have to go right now!" Will said urgently.

"Okay, come on," Marisa agreed. They walked quickly toward the direction of the front entrance until they reached a place where the hallway branched off in two directions. "Uh-oh! Which way to the front?" Marisa asked Will.

He thought about the problem for a moment, then said, "I think we should go through the Hall of North American Forests." They rushed into the hall that displayed giant sequoia trees and instantly realized that it didn't look familiar.

"This isn't the right way," said Marisa, frowning.

They hurried back to the spot where the hallways branched and went in the other direction, entering an area with reptile exhibits that Will hadn't yet seen. "Look at that snake!" he shouted. He dashed over to a display about pythons.

"Did you forget we have to find the lobby so we won't . . . ," Marisa began.

Before she could finish, Will was on to the alligator display. "This alligator has eighty teeth," Will said. "Look at how sharp they are."

"We'd better hurry before the museum closes," Marisa reminded him again, "or we're going to be in big trouble."

They raced down several hallways, then went downstairs until they found a door that led them to the museum's lobby.

When they peered through a window in the door, they saw that the lobby was vacant.

"Where is everybody?" Marisa asked confused.

Will pulled on the door. "It's locked!"

"No way," Marisa said, refusing to believe it. She pulled on the door, but it didn't budge.

"We need to find a guard so we can get out of here," Will suggested.

As they headed back the way they had just come, they heard voices in the distance.

"I'm positive the voices are coming from over there," Marisa said, pointing toward the elevator at the end of the hallway.

"Hurry!" Will said. "Let's catch up with them." They dashed down the hall.

"Hey!" Marisa called, as her eyes went wide with alarm watching the elevator doors close. "We missed them," she sighed.

"Let's find someone else," Will said.

"Where should we look?" asked Marisa.

"Earlier, I saw a guard by the monarch butterfly exhibit," Will suggested. "Let's go there." He pushed the elevator button for UP.

Just as Marisa and Will stepped out of the elevator, something fluttered past their heads. They threw up their arms and ducked.

"What's flying around?" Marisa asked as she cautiously peered up at the ceiling along with Will. They could hardly believe what they were seeing. "They're orange butterflies!" Marisa cried.

"They're Monarch butterflies," Will said. "I saw them in the display when I was here before. They were right over. . . ." He stopped short, staring at a completely empty display case. "Where did the butterflies go?" Will cried.

"They just flew down the hall," Marisa said.

"No, I mean the butterflies that were in the display case," Will said, looking puzzled.

"Maybe someone took them out to clean the case," she answered, reasonably.

"Well, there's no one here," Will replied.

Marisa was beginning to feel very nervous. "Let's go see if there's someone in the Hall of Primates," she suggested.

"We have to go through the Hall of African Mammals to get there," Will recalled.

When they entered the hall downstairs, they noticed another empty area, this time the savannah diorama. "I don't believe it!" Will gasped. "Look down there!"

Chapter 3
The Past Comes Alive

"Unbelievable," Marisa whispered. Just in front of them, a herd of real zebras grazed on grasses that were growing from the floor.

Marisa and Will crept down the hall until they were situated among the zebras. Because the animals paid no attention to them, Will asked, "Do you think they're real?"

"They sure smell real," Marisa said.

"Listen," Will said, hushing her. "What's that noise?" A scratchy sound made them both turn around to spy a mother lioness lounging with her cub on top of another empty case.

"This is amazing," Marisa said, "but it just can't be happening. Can two people experience the same dream at the same time?"

"We're not asleep, so we can't be dreaming," Will said, pinching himself to be sure. "If we went to the dinosaur exhibits, do you think we might see an actual living prehistoric animal?"

Marisa's eyes lit up as she said, "Probably, and wouldn't that be cool?"

"Then we can tell everyone that we've seen a real dinosaur," agreed Will.

They quickly ran to the elevator and went back up to the second floor. "It's pretty quiet up here," Marisa noticed as they carefully stepped out into the hall.

Suddenly, Will grabbed Marisa's arm and yanked her back against the wall as two very large Stegosaurs ambled down the hall. The floor shook as they stomped by.

"Thanks, that was close," she gasped.

"No problem," said Will as they watched the many-plated dinosaurs clomp by. In the next second, a powerful wind began blowing, and a crested *Pteranodon* swooped down the hall. Its massive wings brushed the walls as it glided toward them. As it flapped its wings again, it created a wind that knocked Marisa and Will down.

Marisa struggled to sit up, her hands pressed to the floor. She appeared frightened as she said, "Feel the floor. It's shaking again!"

"I wonder what's going on," said Will. In the next second, a huge *Tyrannosaurus rex* stomped toward them.

"Didn't you say that *T. rex* is a meat eater?" shouted Marisa, as the floor rumbled.

"Uh-huh," Will said, swallowing hard.

The *T. rex* paused, sniffed the air, and then bent so low that Marisa and Will could sense its hot breath ruffling their hair. They cringed, trembling, as the *T. rex* roared.

Marisa and Will desperately tried not to move, hoping the beast wouldn't notice them. However, when the *T. rex* blasted them with another deafening roar, they were on their feet. They sprinted back the way they had come.

"Head to the elevator!" Will shouted. He figured that if they could get inside the elevator, they would be safe. The *T. rex* lifted one enormous leg and started after them.

"This way!" Marisa yelled as she yanked Will in the opposite direction. They raced down another hallway, traveling so fast that they barely noticed the sign at the entrance to the Hall of Great Explorations.

"Watch out!" Will yelled as a man wearing a frontier buckskin outfit stepped out in front of them. Unable to stop, Will and Marisa charged right into him.

"Mister, please help!" Marisa cried, as she saw the *T. rex* charge down the hallway, still chasing them. "Hide us! That thing is going to eat us!"

Without saying a word, the man picked up Will and Marisa, one under each arm. Then he began marching straight toward the dinosaur.

Chapter 4
The Great Explorers

Will estimated that the *T. rex* was only three giant thundering steps away from them. Will and Marisa expected the man to dump them in front of the dinosaur. Instead, he carried them into an exhibit of painted woodland scenery, then he took them to a canoe that sat on the bank of a realistically painted river. The *T. rex* roared.

"I think he's angry," Marisa said, cringing.

"Have no worry," the man finally said. "Like all else in this museum, even the water becomes active at times." As he spoke, he dragged the canoe to the river. "Please get in," he invited.

Will and Marisa hesitated until they saw the _T. rex_ coming closer. They decided that anything would be less dangerous than the dinosaur, so they jumped into the canoe, and the man paddled out into a rushing river. To their amazement, the water snatched them away from the angry _T. rex_.

"Are you saying that everything in this museum comes alive after it closes?" Marisa asked.

"That depends," the man answered as he paddled. "Everything comes alive, but only for people with well-developed imaginations. Those fortunate few can truly experience the wonders of the museum. Not often, however, do any of those fortunate few manage to remain after the museum closes. You two are rare indeed," he continued.

A second canoe pulled up alongside them. Another man was paddling it, and a Native American woman sat in the front.

"Captain Lewis," called the man in the second canoe. "Our guide, Sacagawea, said that we have come upon the territory inhabited by her people, the Shoshone. Should we trade with them for horses so we can explore inland?"

"Lewis? Sacagawea?" Will asked. "Are you the Lewis and Clark who explored western America in 1804?"

"We are making this journey at the request of President Thomas Jefferson," Captain Lewis said. "Clark and I are the first U.S. citizens to see these beautiful lands. Do you care to join the expedition?"

Will and Marisa stared at each other, then Will replied, "We need to get to the entrance of the museum so we can get out of here."

"Will is right," Marisa agreed, "but thanks for saving us from the dinosaur, Captain Lewis. Good luck with your expedition."

The captain nodded. Although he looked disappointed, he paddled back to shore.

When they got out of the canoe, Will said,
"We have to find our way to the lobby. Our
class is probably waiting in the bus, and I'm
sure we're in trouble for not being with them."

"I'm more worried about being eaten," Marisa
stated, looking behind her. She thought about
their close call with the *T. rex*.

Will thought for a moment. "Let's go the
other way," he said. "Follow me. I think this
way might be safe."

They located the elevator and went back to the first floor. They walked until they entered the Hall of Primates. "Listen to that noise," Will said.

The hall was alive with the chattering and calls of many different types of monkeys. As they came to the exhibit of gorillas, the racket died down. Like everything else in the museum, the apes had come to life, but they were mostly silent creatures that moved about quietly.

"Marisa, look up in that tree!" Will pointed.

"It's a nest made of leaves," Marisa said.

Will slowly started climbing up the tree. "Will, what are you doing?" Marisa called.

"I have to see this!" he shouted back.

Marisa hesitated and then followed Will up the tree. When they reached the nest, they awkwardly climbed into it.

A gentle snore immediately alerted them to the fact that they were not alone in the leafy nest. "How sweet," Marisa cooed at the sleeping baby gorilla. "I think that this is the cutest thing I've ever seen!" she gushed.

"It is very cool," Will agreed. He smiled down at the baby gorilla as it opened its big brown eyes.

Marisa lifted the gorilla and sat it on her lap, bouncing it gently. Suddenly, she and Will heard grunting noises above their heads, and they both looked up anxiously. A huge face stared down at them from the top of the nest. It was the mother gorilla, and she did not look pleased.

Marisa and Will froze in fear. "What do we do now?" Marisa whispered.

"I have absolutely no idea," Will whispered back, nearly choking.

Chapter 5
The Gorilla Goes Bananas

The mother gorilla slammed her fist between Will and Marisa. They rolled away in opposite directions as the baby scrambled up onto its mother's shoulder.

They quickly climbed down the tree, but the ape was right behind them. When they reached the bottom, the kids moved swiftly away from the tree, not certain where they should go.

Marisa and Will decided to start running. They ran until Will stopped to pull on the doors leading to the Hall of Ocean Life. "They're locked," he reported. Peering in through the window at the top of the door, he called, "Look at this."

Marisa's jaw dropped as she realized that the inside of the Hall of Ocean Life was filled with water. Sea creatures of all kinds were swimming around, including a giant squid that wiggled its many tentacles. They glanced down the hall and realized that the gorilla would probably catch up to them at any moment.

They quickly moved further down the hall. "Let's try this door," Marisa suggested as she frantically pulled on another door. It opened and they slipped inside.

"Lock it," she cried. As they fumbled with the lock, the door was suddenly pushed forward, then splintered and broke. They jumped back as the mother gorilla charged inside.

Screaming, they backed up to the far wall that was actually some kind of panel board full of dials, controls, and switches. The two friends leaned against the controls, cringing in fear.

The mother gorilla lumbered toward them. They ducked out of the way, crashing against a second door next to the control panel. "This door must lead to the Hall of Ocean Life," Marisa yelled.

"We can't go in there. It's full of water," Will shouted back.

They turned around just in time to see the mother gorilla make a giant leap. She landed in front of them and raised her powerful arms.

At that moment, a gigantic tentacle broke through the second door, flailing wildly in all directions. Ocean water began spraying into the control room from the Hall of Ocean Life.

The force of the incoming water pushed back the mother gorilla and her baby. Soaking wet, the mother retreated and sloshed out of the control room through the first door, with her terrified baby still holding onto her shoulder. The water poured after her into the hall.

"Let's get out of here," Will shouted as the water continued to spray into the room, drenching them. Will and Marisa battled their way through the gushing water to try to escape. Just when they had reached the door, the tentacle wrapped itself tightly around Will's body.

"Will!" Marisa screamed as the tentacle pulled him back through the hole in the second door and into the watery Hall of Ocean Life.

Chapter 6

Water All Around

"Help!" Marisa screamed. She tried to catch one of Will's feet. She managed to grab one ankle, but it slid through her hand as if it had been greased. She watched helplessly through the hole in the door as the giant squid's tentacle squeezed her friend tighter and tighter. She had never seen Will with such a red face or terrified expression.

The amount of water coming through the hole increased. "We need help!" Marisa shouted again just before she was swept off her feet by the powerful force. *If only Lewis and Clark were here*, she frantically thought. *We never should have left them.*

Marisa struggled to her feet, but she couldn't move forward because the gushing water kept pushing her back against the control panel. Then she slipped and fell. As she struggled to regain her feet before she drowned, her hand slammed against a button on the control panel.

Suddenly, a voice filled the room, and Marisa realized it was speaking throughout the entire museum. It was the same recorded voice that had announced that the museum was closing.

Instead of saying the museum was closing, it announced something different. "It is nine o'clock, and the Museum of Natural History is now open for visitors."

A guard, who was about ready to start his nightly walk around the museum, heard the announcement. "What?" he said, as he had a terrible thought. *The museum just closed, so that must mean that someone is messing around with the controls. There's an intruder in the museum!* He sprinted toward the control room.

In the control room, the water had stopped rushing through the door and had slowed to a trickle. Then it suddenly stopped. Marisa stood shakily, trying to catch her breath. At that moment, the guard burst into the room.

"Who are you? What are you doing in here?" the guard demanded sternly. Then he stared at Marisa with a puzzled look and asked, "Why are you all wet?"

Marisa looked at one door and then at the other. There was no hole in the door, no giant tentacle waving around, no water anywhere.

She suddenly remembered that Captain Lewis had said the museum comes to life only for people with good imaginations. *The guard must not have a good imagination*, she thought.

Cautiously, Marisa looked into the Hall of Ocean Life. Everything was calm and still again, but where was Will?

Suddenly, Marisa heard Will yelling, "Help! Somebody pleeeease get me down from here! It's too far to jump!"

Following the direction of the voice, Marisa and the guard looked up. Far above them they spotted Will, hanging by his shirt from one of the giant squid's long tentacles. The squid wasn't moving; it was once again a model.

"How on earth did he get up there?" the puzzled guard asked Marisa.

"It's a long story," replied Marisa, as she pulled on the bottom of her shirt and began to wring it out. A puddle formed on the floor.

The guard wanted to hear what Marisa had to say, but decided that getting the boy down was more important at the moment. He told Marisa that he would get a ladder and that she was not to move because he wanted an explanation.

As the guard left the room, Marisa shouted up to Will, "Hang on! He'll be right back!"

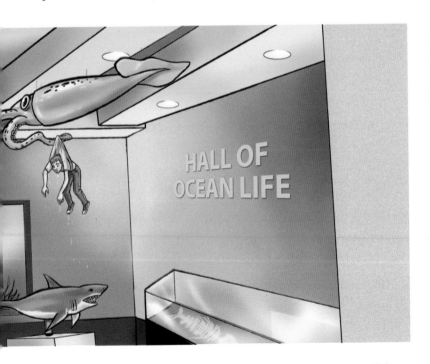

HALL OF
OCEAN LIFE

"He'd better hurry!" screamed Will. "I don't think that this shirt is strong enough to hold me much longer."

As she stared upward, Marisa heard a faint ripping sound. Suddenly, she had a terrible thought. *Now that the guard had left the room, what if the squid and everything else comes back to life?* All of a sudden, she saw one of the squid's tentacles twitch. She wasn't sure if she could trust her eyes, but then the tentacles twitched again.

Marisa was about to warn Will, when the guard came rushing back in carrying a ladder, and everything was quiet once more. She sighed with relief.

"Stand back," the guard told Marisa, as he carefully began setting up the ladder.

The guard scaled the tall ladder and carefully pulled on Will's shirt. It wasn't an easy task, but he finally managed to lift Will off the tentacle without dropping him.

"Way to go!" Marisa cheered as the guard and Will climbed down.

As soon as they were safely off the ladder, Will bent down and kissed the ground. Marisa began laughing, until she noticed the guard wasn't laughing with her. In fact, he had a very angry expression on his face. *Uh, oh!* she thought.

"You two have some explaining to do," the guard demanded. Marisa and Will looked at each other, knowing they were in big trouble. How could they ever explain what had happened, especially since there seemed to be no evidence around them that would even prove why they were wet. The room was completely dry. If they hadn't been wet, Will and Marisa wondered whether they could even trust their own imaginations. Had it all really happened?

Chapter 7

Fifteen Minutes

The guard led Marisa and Will to his office. As they were walking, they went through the Hall of Hominids. As she gazed around and saw the skeletons behind the glass cases, Marisa shuddered.

She whispered to Will, "I'm glad we weren't in *this* hall when everything came to life."

Will stared at her and shivered in return.

When they got to the office, the guard sat them down and told them to start explaining. Just as Marisa was about to begin, they heard pounding on the museum's front doors.

The guard got up and went to see who it was. When he opened the door, Ms. Baker rushed in looking frantic. Without stopping to pause in between sentences, she said, "When we got to the bus, two of my students were missing. They were supposed to be with the rest of the class."

The guard told her to follow him, and he brought her into the office. When she saw Will and Marisa, she ran over and gave them a big hug. Then she stepped back and asked, "Why weren't you two with the rest of the class when the museum closed? Where have you been? Why are you wet? I've been worried sick about you for the last 15 minutes. I couldn't even begin to imagine how I was going to tell the school and your families that I had lost two students."

Marisa and Will asked at the same time, "Fifteen minutes?" They looked at each other, completely confused. They had been trying to get out of the museum for a lot longer than 15 minutes; it had been hours and hours!

"The museum has been closed for a lot longer than 15 minutes," said Marisa to the guard and Ms. Baker.

"What are you talking about, Marisa?" asked Ms. Baker, looking very puzzled.

"For all of the adventures we've had, it feels like we've been in here for hours," Will said.

"What kind of adventures?" asked the guard, suspiciously.

Will began to explain how the door to the lobby was locked when they got there.

"We tried to find someone to let us out," Marisa chimed in.

Together, Will and Marisa related seeing the butterflies and the zebras, meeting Lewis and Clark, being chased by the dinosaur, and finding the baby gorilla in the nest. Then they ran from the mother, and were nearly drowned and squeezed to death by the squid.

"Wait!" Ms. Baker held up her hands to stop the torrent of words. "You two are already in trouble for not joining the rest of the class when it was time to go," Ms. Baker said sternly. "Making up an outrageous story like that is just going to get you into more trouble."

"We're not making it up," Marisa insisted.

"Yeah, you should have seen the gorilla chasing us," Will added. "How could we make up something like that?"

"Why aren't the exhibits alive now?" asked the guard, still not believing their story.

"Captain Lewis told us that the museum only comes to life for people who possess good imaginations," answered Marisa.

"Captain Lewis?" asked Ms. Baker.

"You know, Lewis and Clark," said Will, "the explorers from the 1800s."

Ms. Baker said, "Well, I'm glad you know your history, but I'm still going to have to tell your parents what happened."

"Look over there!" Marisa shouted. "It's the monarch butterflies from the exhibit."

They all turned to look. Marisa and Will noticed Captain Lewis standing in the shadows near the butterfly exhibit. He raised his hand and waved it slightly.

Ms. Baker was staring at the butterflies. "They're alive!" she gasped.

"What's alive?" asked the puzzled guard.

Will and Marisa smiled at each other. Ms. Baker would *have* to believe their story now. Best of all, they had always suspected she had a good imagination. Now they knew.

The Museum Chase

By Suzanne Weyn

Illustrated by James Elston

CELEBRATION PRESS
Pearson Learning Group

Contents